THE
PLC at Work™
Cartoon Book

Cartoons by Martha F. Campbell
Foreword by Richard DuFour & Rebecca DuFour

Solution Tree | Press
a division of
Solution Tree

555 North Morton Street

Bloomington, IN 47404

800.733.6786 (toll free) / 812.336.7700

FAX: 812.336.7790

email: info@solution-tree.com

solution-tree.com

Visit **go.solution-tree.com/plcbooks** to download a selection of the cartoons.

Printed in the United States of America

15   14   13   3   4   5

Library of Congress Cataloging-in-Publication Data

Campbell, Martha (Martha F.)

  The PLC at Work Cartoon Book / Martha Campbell.

     p. cm.

  Includes bibliographical references.

  ISBN 978-1-935543-09-1 (perfect bound)

  1. Professional learning communities--Caricatures and cartoons. 2. American wit and humor, Pictorial. I. Title.

  NC1429.C2857A4 2011

  741.5'6973--dc22

                              2010050706

Solution Tree

Jeffrey C. Jones, CEO & President

Solution Tree Press

President: Douglas M. Rife

Publisher: Robert D. Clouse

Vice President of Production: Gretchen Knapp

Managing Production Editor: Caroline Wise

Copy Editor: Rachel Rosolina

Proofreader: Elisabeth Abrams

Text and Cover Designer: Jenn Taylor

Table of Contents

About the Artist

Martha F. Campbell is a graduate of the School of Fine Arts, Washington University, St. Louis, and a former writer and designer for Hallmark Cards. She has been a freelance cartoonist and illustrator since leaving Hallmark. She lives in Harrison, Arkansas.

About the DuFours

Richard DuFour, EdD, is the author of many books and has written numerous professional articles. He was a public school educator for thirty-four years, serving as a teacher, principal, and superintendent. He consults with school districts, state departments, and professional organizations throughout North America on strategies for improving schools.

Rebecca DuFour consults with and works for professional organizations, school districts, universities, and state departments of education throughout North America. She has written for numerous professional journals and has served as a teacher, school administrator, and central office coordinator.

Foreword

Richard DuFour and Rebecca DuFour

Over the course of many years, we have written about the challenge of transforming traditional schools into professional learning communities (PLCs). We have cautioned that those who engage in this process will be called upon to demonstrate a sense of moral purpose, clarity of vision, a willingness to collaborate with others in an important collective endeavor, vulnerability, risk taking, an action orientation, and a commitment to using evidence of student learning to drive continuous improvement. We have warned educators that this transformation will require perseverance, tenacity, and courage. This all sounds very serious and somber.

What we sometimes forget to emphasize, however, is that those who engage in this important work must maintain a sense of humor and the ability to laugh at themselves, so they can keep moving forward when things don't work out as planned—and things never work out as planned. Most of us are familiar with Murphy's Law: "Whatever can go wrong, will go wrong." In the early stages of implementing the PLC process, you will discover that Murphy was an optimist. There is no concept or process so powerful that it can be executed flawlessly if it involves people. Add school-aged children as a factor, and the challenges of effective implementation increase exponentially.

Martha Campbell does a wonderful job of illustrating the reactions to the PLC process from the perspective of principals, teachers, and students. She combines her understanding of professional learning communities, her insights into human nature, and her wonderful sense of humor to create a work that reminds us that changing the structure and culture of a school is not a neat, rational, linear systematic process. It is messy, it is irrational, it is random. It is, as Michael Fullan so aptly describes, "just one damn thing after another." Campbell gently urges us to embrace the mess and see the humor in it.

We provide an introductory overview of each section of the book, which highlights a key term and concept of the PLC at Work™ process. Some of the cartoons made us smile, others made us chuckle, and many made us laugh out loud. We are confident you will appreciate Campbell's wit and wisdom. So enjoy, and remember to keep both your faith in the benefits of the PLC at Work process and your sense of humor as you move forward on the journey.

Visit **go.solution-tree.com/plcbooks** to download a selection of the cartoons.

Learning for All

Peruse the mission statement of virtually every school district in North America, and you will find that the mission is grounded in a commitment to help all students learn. Unfortunately, too often an enormous gap exists between those lofty mission statements and the actual practices of schools, particularly when students do not learn. In a 2009 *MetLife Survey of the American Teacher* by Dana Markow and Andrea Pieters, 100 percent of teachers who participated reported that they were confident in their knowledge and skills to help all students learn. Almost two-thirds of those same teachers, however, acknowledged that they did not expect their students to learn. Their assumption was, "We are okay, but the kids are not okay. We have all the skills to be effective, but the teachers who prepared the students for our course or grade level were ineffective, or perhaps the students lack parental support."

We attempted to capture this sentiment in the following poem, "It's Not My Fault," which first appeared in *Revisiting Professional Learning Communities at Work*™ (DuFour, DuFour, & Eaker, 2008, pp. 417–418).

It's Not My Fault

"He doesn't have the skills we need,"
the employer harrumphed with disgust.
"The colleges are ivory towers
so training him falls to us."

"It's not our fault," the professors cried.
"He was deficient in every way.
Remediation has become our task
because high schools fail kids today."

"But kids we get can't read or write.
He didn't know things he should.
We high school teachers aren't at fault.
The middle school's no damn good."

"We can't overcome six years of neglect,"
the middle school teachers explained.
"If elementary schools won't do their job,
then they're the ones to blame."

"He wasn't school ready when he arrived,"
the K–5 teachers moaned.
"All we can do is babysit.
The fault lies in the home."
"It's really not the poor dear's fault,"
his mother was heard to say.
"He's a victim of his family tree . . .
His father's the same way."

The first step in demonstrating a commitment to helping all kids
learn requires educators to focus on their own spheres of influence.
Parents are not leaving the good kids at home. These are the kids!
Let's ensure that they all learn.

"Then that's four votes to establish a professional learning community, and one 'it's not enough to succeed . . . others must fail.'"

"I don't think you're trying hard enough to see things from the perspective of the unlearned, Ms. Diaz."

"The first little pig built his house of straw, the second little pig built his house of sticks, and the third little pig built a PLC."

"Behind every PLC is a veteran teacher rolling his eyes."

"Way to shift the blame."

"I understand they had a rather spirited meeting this morning."

"I thought that was *our* job."

"Yes, Robert, you're all going to graduate, but this isn't a diploma mill."

"I think I'm a gifted student, Mom. We're only on *JKL*, but the teachers have already told me to watch my *P*s and *Q*s."

"Yes, Eduardo. I'm sure that if you devour all that knowledge, you won't be too full for lunch."

"We can't say they aren't learning. Twenty-three of them have learned to call in sick."

"Mrs. Kim always said she'd go to the ends of the earth to see that we learned, and that's where she went."

"We are assuming collective responsibility for your learning, Kenny, not ganging up on you."

Collaboration

Public education in the United States began in one-room school-houses in which a single adult, working in isolation, was solely responsible for the learning of every student in the room. Unfortunately, that condition continues, as many schools are, in effect, a series of one-room schoolhouses located under the same roof. This isolation has not been foisted upon educators: they have embraced it. We frequently ask groups of educators if they can complete the following sentence, because they have either said it or heard it in their own schools: "I wish they would just give me my room, give me my kids, and . . ." Without fail, they roar in choral response, "LEAVE ME ALONE!"

The idea that a single teacher working in isolation can meet the diverse needs of every student in his or her classroom has not worked in the past and certainly will not work in the future. A single principal working in isolation cannot successfully fulfill the myriad challenges of leadership. Breaking the tradition of isolation and learning to work in consort will not be easy, but it is essential if educators are to succeed in the incredibly complex task of helping all students learn.

Organizing isolated individuals into groups will not be sufficient. Educators will need time to collaborate as well as the training and support to ensure that their collective efforts are focused on the right work. Co-laboring on the wrong tasks will do nothing to improve student achievement. Mona Mourshed, Chinezi Chijioke, and Michael Barber, in their study *How the World's Most Improved School Systems Keep Getting Better*, found that the collaborative efforts of those schools were "all about teachers and school leaders working together to develop effective instructional practices, studying what works well in classrooms, and doing so both with rigorous attention to detail and with a commitment to improving not only one's own practice but that of others. . . . This is the essence of collaborative practice: teachers jointly engaged in an empirical, routine, and applied study of their own profession" (2010, pp. 84–85). So ask yourself two questions: "Has my school organized the staff to ensure that we work interdependently in a collaborative and collective effort to fulfill a common purpose, or are we organized into independent kingdoms staffed by relatively autonomous subcontractors who work in isolation? When I collaborate with my colleagues, is our work focused on improving our individual and adult practice in order to get better results for the students we serve?"

"You'd be expected to be a team player in any job,
Ms. Ramos, but here we really mean it."

"Collaboration would be a lot easier if it weren't
for all those collaborators."

"I think our collaborative culture needs work, don't you . . . Sam . . . and Jane?"

"I don't know about you, but I for one give up
trying to get Ed to participate."

"Probably an early vertical team."

"This is just the kind of isolation we're trying to avoid, Ms. Moore."

"In a burst of enthusiasm, I yelled, 'Go, team, go!'

. . . and they left."

"Enforcing the norms has been a lot easier since I thought of using the mute."

"Go away, Miguel. This team doesn't need anyone
to provide the play by play."

"We're beginning to form a cohesive faculty. This is my colleague, Maria."

"Bill here has some sort of complaint about the refreshments at the team meetings, sir."

"There's a bully on my team."

"The janitor requests that we let the principal in.
He's tired of cleaning the window."

"You'd think the teachers in this school, of all schools, would be able to tell the difference between talking in class and collaborating."

"I really dread the next meeting."

"There are more productive ways of
resolving conflict, Tom."

Collective Inquiry

Think about all the questions a teacher must consider when preparing a unit of instruction. Some of those questions include:

- What knowledge, skills, and dispositions must students acquire as a result of this unit?

- What instructional strategies will be most effective in helping all students acquire the intended outcomes?

- What is the best way to sequence the content?

- How should I pace instruction?

- How can I gather evidence of student learning as I am teaching?

- What is the best way to assess student learning at the end of the unit?

- What criteria will I use to judge the quality of student work?

- What can I do to provide additional time and support for students who are struggling?

- What can I do to enrich and extend the learning for students who are proficient?

If educators address these questions in isolation, students in the same course or grade level are subject to very different experiences. In a professional learning community, educators address these and other questions *collectively* because collective inquiry is a better way to promote both effectiveness and equity.

One of the most important questions members of a PLC consider is, "Why are we doing this at all?" They are willing to examine both their curriculum and their pedagogy from a critical perspective. They not only establish to-do lists, but they are also willing to consider what to include on a "stop-doing" list.

Perhaps you have heard the story of the wife who would buy a ten-pound roast each week, trim two inches off the end, and then cook the roast. When her husband finally asked why she trimmed the roast, he was told, "Because that is the way you are supposed to cook a roast. Every roast my mother ever cooked, she trimmed two inches off before cooking it." When the husband asked his mother-in-law for an explanation, she explained, "I never had a roasting pan big enough for a ten-pound roast."

Collective inquiry challenges us to go beyond appeals to mindless precedent. "We do it because we have always done it" is not a good rationale. What's on your stop-doing list?

"The teachers do everything collectively. How do we know they're not a cult?"

"We brainstormed."

"They can add digits, subtract digits, multiply and divide digits, but 85 percent of them don't know what a digit is."

"We're addressing our weaknesses. We're addressing them to a school in another city."

"There's only one way all our students are going to pass the state test. We have to get Larry Twohy's mother to homeschool him."

"That's where they go to learn from our mistakes."

"Are you going to show us your bag of tricks or not?"

"Knowing what you want to accomplish is half the battle. The other half is the room full of fourth graders."

"We're not here to express personal opinions, Gerald—yours in particular."

"Has anyone tried reading them *The Little Engine That Could*?"

"My class can't wait to learn multiplication. I made them sign a pledge never to use it for evil purposes."

"That's who the principal thinks I am."

SMART Goals

We had a friend who was convinced that the key to avoiding failure is never setting a goal. In a PLC, however, the very definition of a collaborative team is "people working *interdependently* to achieve a *common goal* for which members are held *mutually accountable*." Note that the pursuit of mutual goals is fundamental to that definition. Furthermore, teams are asked to commit to *SMART* goals. *As opposed to what,* you're wondering . . . *stupid goals?* No, but let's be honest. In traditional schools, educators focus on teaching rather than learning, work alone rather than in teams, and focus on teacher activity rather than student learning. *If* goals are established, they are most often teacher/teaching oriented, rather than student-results oriented. Thus, educators in traditional settings have been famous for establishing, not stupid goals, but rather SMATT goals!

> **S**trategic and specific
>
> **M**easurable
>
> **A**ttainable
>
> **T**eaching oriented
>
> **T**ime bound

In PLCs at Work, traditional SMATT goals such as, "We will adopt a new textbook this year," "I will create three new labs for my science course this quarter," or "I will use cooperative learning more often in my classroom this semester" give way to SMART goals, goals that are (*The Handbook for SMART School Teams*, Conzemius & O'Neill, 2005):

> **S**trategic and specific
>
> **M**easurable
>
> **A**ttainable
>
> **R**esults oriented
>
> **T**ime bound

Examples of SMART goals might include, "We will increase the percentage of students who meet or exceed the state standard in our course from 83 percent last year to at least 90 percent this year," or "We will reduce the failure rate in our course by at least 50 percent from last year to this year." These goals focus on results. In order to achieve them, more students must actually learn at higher levels.

The SMART goal process calls upon teams to identify the current level of student learning, establish a goal to improve upon that level, develop and implement an action plan to achieve the goal, gather periodic evidence of progress, celebrate improvement, and begin again more intelligently if the team falls short of its goal.

SMART goals can help transform a group of educators into a team, can shift their focus from activity to results, and can provide a basis for frequent celebration of progress. Most importantly, SMART goals reflect an explicit commitment to help more students learn at higher levels.

"Never tell them a goal is like a target."

"I don't know if it was a stretch goal, son. I just
know the cow jumped over the moon."

"I don't think giving it the old college try is an attainable goal, Miss Vargas. I'm only in middle school."

"We could learn something about stretch goals
from Eddie."

"This, Robert, is definitely an attainable goal."

"Just for fun, let's set a couple of
unattainable ones."

"I know I can train them to be thoughtful, productive citizens if I can ever get past *sit*. The getting past *sit* part is specific but unattainable."

"Getting your homework done in time to watch *Dancing With the Stars* is time bound, Beverly, but not smart."

"Turns out 'make them smart' isn't a SMART goal."

"If they acquire the wisdom of Solomon, will we
have violated the separation of church and state?"

"My goal for tonight is purposeless, ambiguous, immeasurable, unaccounted-for TV viewing for as long as I feel like it. I think that's attainable."

"You don't think it's too ambitious, do you?"

Action Orientation

Members of PLCs are action oriented: they learn by doing. They understand that the most powerful learning always occurs in a context of taking action. In fact, the very reason that educators work together in teams and engage in collective inquiry is to serve as catalysts for action. They recognize that until members of the organization "do" differently, there is no reason to anticipate different results. They avoid paralysis through analysis and overcome inertia with action.

In our work with schools, we have found that some educators are adept at finding substitutes for action. They form committees to study a problem. They read books about the problem. They attend training sessions about the problem. They have faculty dialogues concerning the problem. They develop strategic plans that articulate the problem. What they *don't* do is take specific actions to resolve the problem.

In PLCs, educators build shared knowledge and then immediately translate that knowledge into action. They try a lot of things, learn what works and what does not work, think about what they learned, and then try again with the deeper insights that come from experience.

There is an old joke that asks, "Eight frogs are on a log. Five decide to jump into the pond. How many frogs are left on the log?" The correct answer is, "Eight, because there is a difference between deciding to do something and actually doing it."

The joke reminds us of our colleague and best friend, Bob Eaker, who is fond of using the word *fixin'*. Bob will say, "I'm fixin' to write . . . I'm fixin' to take a trip . . . I'm fixin' to mow the lawn." We tease him that *fixin'* is just another word for *procrastination*. We insist that either he is writing or he is not writing. If he wants to write, write. We offer the same challenge to readers. Don't fall into the trap of fixin' to become a PLC. To paraphrase the wise philosopher Yoda: Do, or do not. . . . There is no fixin'. Your deepest learning about the PLC process will occur when you begin doing what PLCs actually do.

"I know we're supposed to be action oriented, but
I resent the motion detectors."

"This is good. We're definitely moving out of our comfort zone."

"Today we practice learning by doing. Please open the boxes containing action figures of yourselves."

"The Picasso boy is doing very well, but let's call his mother in anyway. I really want to meet her."

"You wouldn't know it by looking, but they're really pretty action oriented."

"Notify the faculty that we're changing the schedule,
but grief counselors will be provided."

"If doing something were really better than doing nothing, where would La-Z-Boy be?"

"Look at these satellite pictures. You can see our knowing-doing gap from space."

"You knew the road to hell was paved with good
intentions when you established that PLC."

Intervention

Imagine entering a Burger King only to find it is out of burgers. This would strike you as odd. You would reason that certainly an organization whose very mission is to sell burgers to the public would have systems in place for monitoring the burger inventory and a well-thought-out plan for ensuring additional burgers would be forthcoming if the inventory ran low. If for some reason the plan failed to acquire the burgers in a timely fashion, there would be additional steps in the plan that would reflect the increasing urgency of the situation. This misalignment between the mission of Burger King and processes to ensure that the mission could be addressed would be puzzling indeed.

Yet in schools throughout North America that proclaim their fundamental mission is to ensure that all students learn, there is no systematic plan for monitoring student learning and no coordinated execution of a well-conceived plan for providing assistance when some students do not learn. This should strike us as, well, odd.

What happens when students do not learn does not depend on the schools they attend, but rather on the randomness of the teachers to whom they are assigned. Some teachers will allow students to retake an examination, while others won't. Some will insist students keep working on a project until it is acceptable, and others will simply assign a failing grade. Some teachers come early or stay late to help their struggling students, and some will not or cannot. Some teachers will consistently fail three times more students than their colleagues teaching the same course. Educators are certainly aware of these variations, and it is not uncommon for them to work with the principal or counselors to ensure their own sons and daughters are not assigned to those teachers who routinely fail high numbers of students. On Wall Street, this would be considered insider trading, and you could go to jail. In many schools, it is considered a professional perk.

Isn't it time we stopped playing educational lottery with kids' lives? Isn't it time that we demonstrate a commitment to ensuring all kids learn by actually having a plan for helping them when they do not learn?

"Miss Albert is very quick to spot trouble. She intervened right between *four plus four* and *equals*."

"They'll have to admit I make it easy for them to know when I'm not learning."

"I'm getting a tutor. You know, a personal trainer
for the brain."

"Dennis Edwards didn't understand multiplication. It took the whole mathematics department, but Dennis Edwards understands multiplication. Now Dennis Edwards doesn't understand division. . . ."

"The pyramid of interventions might make sense to the teachers, but it's all hieroglyphics to me."

"'Give me liberty, or give me death' is the correct Patrick Henry quote, but you still have to spend the afternoon in Homework Club."

"I'm attending an enrichment period today."

"Yes, I know what it adds up to. It adds up to intervention for Eddie Goldbeck."

"Those floating tutors aren't so great. They just stand on the floor like everyone else."

"I tried to call my math mentor, but predictably, I got the wrong number."

"All I said was, 'Correct me if I'm wrong,' and ever since,
it's been success coordinators . . . tutoring centers . . .
study skills classes . . . support groups . . ."

"I'm afraid there's going to be a lot of intervention between *Here's how you do this* and *I get it.*"

"Ignorance is bliss, Ms. Chen. If ignorance is bliss, why do I have to go to intervention?"

"We'd like to work in time for intervention, but our schedule is chiseled in stone, and chiseled in stone at the highest level."

Continuous Improvement

Charles Osgood once described a "pretty good school" with "pretty good students" taught by pretty good teachers "who always let pretty good pass."

It is easy for educators to fall victim to the "pretty good school" syndrome and become content with the status quo. After all, virtually every school district in North America has a valedictorian, honor society members, and a top half of the graduating class. Thus, educators can reason that some kids are doing well, and those who are not must accept responsibility for their low performance.

If the achievement of students in a school happens to be higher than the average achievement in the state, its educators are even more likely to see their school as "good enough." Furthermore, if the school serves a wealthy community where students consistently achieve at high levels on high-stakes tests, it may be particularly difficult to persuade the staff that there is room for improvement. As the old joke goes, "They were born on third and decided they hit a triple."

In a professional learning community, educators recognize that no matter how high students achieve on average, the school is made up of individual students whose parents have hopes and dreams for their children. For a family whose child has had a bad educational experience, the school is a 100 percent failure.

A perpetual discontent with the status quo and a constant search for a better way to reach kids characterize professional learning communities. Educators throughout the school benchmark against themselves and others, and they strive to improve upon previous performance.

We remember seeing a cartoon of a family of nomads crossing the desert on camels, and the father turns to the children and says, "Quit asking if we are almost home yet. We are nomads for crying out loud." Working in a PLC is a lot like that—a wonderful and endless journey.

"I see they left room for improvement."

"They have to keep improving, sir. We have a full box of my-kid-made-the-honor-roll bumper stickers left."

"When you emailed that you wanted to discuss ways to improve results without Homework Club, I thought you were one of the teachers."

"The good news is, the children of the district
have improved their writing skills. The bad news is,
we've been deluged with complaint letters
from the third grade."

"Your students consistently show the most improvement, Ms. Hill. You had to expect to be cloned."

"Well, it's continuous improvement, isn't it?"

"Ninety-five percent of the story problems have happy endings."

"It's one thing for the superintendent of schools to comment on the district's lack of improvement. It's another thing entirely for a member of this faculty to stand up and holler, 'You try it!'"

"They never quit, do they?"

"We asked for all that extra training so we wouldn't really have to *do* anything, and it worked. We're overqualified."

Results

According to Patrick Lencioni's study of teams, inattention to results leads to dysfunctional teams. In PLCs at Work, educators judge their effectiveness on the basis of results, focusing on tangible evidence of intended outcomes rather than on activities or intentions. If the results should happen to be unfavorable, educators in a PLC neither ignore them nor make excuses for them but confront the brutal facts and look for ways to use the information to improve. In other words, educators in PLCs embrace the adage that "knowledge is power," rather than "ignorance is bliss."

In traditional school settings, individual teachers typically use assessment results to prove whether or not students have learned in order to justify the grades they assign. In a PLC, collaborative teams of teachers use results from frequent common formative assessments to *improve* student learning and their own professional practice. Teams analyze the results for three purposes:

1. They identify individual students who need additional time and support for learning. The focus on individual results helps the school monitor student learning by name and by need.

2. They help individual teachers identify strengths and weaknesses in their instruction. If the students of one teacher

struggle to learn a skill or concept compared to similar students taught by one or more teammates, the teacher can call upon his or her colleagues for help in addressing the problem area. If the teacher's students excel, he or she can share effective strategies with colleagues.

3. They enable the team to identify and celebrate improvement in student learning and to explore ideas for helping more students learn a particular skill or concept at a higher level.

So what happens when a team does not achieve its intended results? W. C. Fields advises, "If at first you don't succeed, try again. Then quit. No sense in being a damn fool about it." In a PLC, however, the focus on results provides educators with benchmarks of their progress and informs the next steps on their journey.

"The new data analysis software is here, Ms. Riggs.
Could you send one of the third graders down to
install it?"

"I pray for the answers. It skews the data."

"The eighth graders are good with words. That's what they used to rewrite history."

"All right! Who's been demonstrating mastery of critical writing skills on the weight room wall?"

"There's nothing wrong with this data that a little Wite-Out wouldn't cure."

"This semester's test scores must be worse than we thought. He has a doctorate in English, and all he could come up with was 'Geez . . .'"

"I think we're too dependent on data."

"This is a formative assessment, sir. We need your summative assessment."

"Congratulations, Carlos. I don't believe I've read a more evasive and misleading assessment in all my years in education."

"Common assessments may be all right for the
eighth-grade teachers, but we ninth-grade teachers
pride ourselves on uncommon assessments."

"We're having one of those common assessment
tests tomorrow. You know—one size fits all
except me."

Celebration

Why is being attentive to celebration such an important part of the PLC process?

- **It sustains the improvement process.** When organizational researchers are asked, "What is the most important factor in sustaining an improvement initiative?," their almost-universal response is, "Recognize and celebrate small wins."

- **It addresses a basic human need.** Psychologists acknowledge that few human needs are more basic than to be noticed, recognized, and appreciated for our efforts.

- **It is a powerful way to communicate what is valued.** The word *recognition* comes from the Latin for *to know again*. When educators publicly recognize staff members who personify the purpose and priorities of their schools, they remind everyone of what the school stands for.

As Martha Campbell's cartoons illustrate, however, celebration can be done badly when it is not specifically tied to the purpose and priorities of the school, and it can be divisive rather than unifying if it is limited to one or two individuals. To use celebration effectively, consider the following:

- **Constantly remind people of the purpose of celebration.** Celebration is a powerful tool for sustaining momentum by recognizing incremental progress, creating an environment with frequent expressions of appreciation and admiration, and reminding the entire staff of the priorities of the school and the collective commitments to achieve those values. As Kouzes and Posner write in *Encouraging the Heart*, "Celebration is the symbolic adhesive that wields a community together. . . . Celebration serves as the organization's heart" (1999, p. 114).

- **Make celebration everyone's responsibility.** If the formal leader is the sole arbiter of who will be recognized, the rest of the staff can merely sit back and critique the choices. Every staff member should have the opportunity to publicly acknowledge his or her appreciation and admiration for the work of a colleague.

- **Establish a clear link between the recognition and the behavior or commitment you are attempting to encourage and reinforce.** Recognition should always be accompanied with a story relating the efforts of the team or individual back to the core foundation of the school or district. Celebration should provide others with an example they can emulate.

- **Create opportunities to have many winners.** Celebration will not have a significant effect on the culture of a school if most people in the organization feel they have no opportunity to be recognized. The most important criterion of public recognition is the sincerity with which it is given, and we need not place caps or quotas on sincere appreciation. Design your celebrations to create many winners, and have fun doing it!

"We need to choose somebody to plan a little celebration. Did anyone here go to a party school?"

"They're good! Even their celebrations are time bound."

"It does recognize three teachers rather than one,
but resentment could crop up."

"It was the week he taught the chapter on global climate change."

"That's going to lessen the impact of the little celebration we had planned for him at school."

"She'll like it. She'll count off for spelling, but she'll like it."

"There's a celebration carried way too far."

"Do you have a plain 'Congratulations, Teacher of the Week'? We don't want success to go to her head."

"It's a little appreciation gift from the principal."

"I'm here to congratulate you, Ms. Rios. All your students tell me they make straight As."

"First we accomplish something, Ed. *Then* we celebrate."

"I understand there was some disagreement over
the selection."

"Philip is moving out of the district, and that calls
for a celebration, which we'll refer to as a going
away party."

Head of the Class
Phi Delta Kappa International
Treat yourself and your colleagues to a healthy dose of laughter with this compilation of the best cartoons ever published in *Phi Delta Kappan.*
BKF328

Learning by Doing, Second Edition
Richard DuFour, Rebecca DuFour, Robert Eaker, and Thomas Many
The second edition of this pivotal action guide includes seven major additions that equip educators with essential tools for confronting challenges.
BKF416

A Leader's Companion
Robert Eaker, Rebecca DuFour, and Richard DuFour
Treat yourself to daily moments of reflection with inspirational quotes collected from a decade of work by renowned professional learning community experts.
BKF227

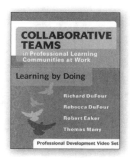

Collaborative Teams in Professional Learning Communities at Work™
Richard DuFour, Rebecca DuFour, Robert Eaker, and Thomas Many
This short program shows exactly what collaborative teams do. Aligned with the best-selling book *Learning by Doing*, the video features unscripted footage of collaboration in action.
DVF023

Solution Tree | Press

a division of
Solution Tree

Visit solution-tree.com or call 800.733.6786 to order.

Wait! Your professional development journey doesn't have to end with the last pages of this book.

We realize improving student learning doesn't happen overnight. And your school or district shouldn't be left to puzzle out all the details of this process alone.

No matter where you are on the journey, we're committed to helping you get to the next stage.

Take advantage of everything from **custom workshops** to **keynote presentations** and **interactive web and video conferencing**. We can even help you develop an action plan tailored to fit your specific needs.

Let's get the conversation started.

Call 888.763.9045 today.